SO YOU'RE GOING OFF TO COLLEGE:

DON'T FORGET YOUR SURVIVAL GUIDE FOR FIRST YEAR FRESHMEN

BY DR. ZOE SPENCER

"I want to go to a place where I can drink from the fountain of knowledge."

Learning is an experience that should benefit both the teacher and the student. It is an opportunity to explore and seek the knowledge that will nourish your growth and development, your progress, and most importantly your consciousness. The process of learning should not be taken lightly. Instead, it should be embraced as an integral part of your being that is required for you to write the beautiful life "chapters-after" that you deserve. Every situation, good and bad, is an opportunity to learn. Every learning experience is an opportunity to grow. So, learn and grow...evolve...transform and then emerge from this journey greater than before.

You have arrived at the "fountain" - that is your University. Allow your professors to pour knowledge into your cup, sip. As you build-pour your knowledge into our cups and into our community. Let's toast...To the beauty that knowledge is and the consciousness that it builds.

Welcome to VSU! Loving you already! Dr. Z

INTRODUCTION

So, you've made it. You've successfully completed high school, gotten through those God awful SAT's or ACT's or CAT's and DOG's, with a score decent enough to get you into college. Or perhaps you've chosen a college that understands that the 4 and a half hours that it took you to sit for the standardized test, and the amount of money that your parents paid to "prep" you for the stupid test, doesn't actualize or reflect your entire 14 years of academic growth and achievement, nor does it determine your future potential as a successful college student. Whatever the case, you've been accepted into college. You've made it and you're on your way. Congratulations!

Now begins a completely new phase of your life-a new scene, a new routine. A new routine that offers you a taste of independence that you've probably been longing for since you could think rationally. This is the opportunity for you to be away from the rigid micro-management of your parents, older siblings, community and church members, former teachers, and principals.

You can now go to bed when you want, eat what you want, watch and listen to what you want, go where you want, come home (that is back to the dorm) when you want, and even drink and smoke when you want. But more significantly to the academic experience, you can now make your own academic decisions.

Yes, even though there is a routine-a curriculum, that if not followed, could cause you to stay in college an extra year or two or three, you can technically create your own academic schedule-write your own ticket. And even if you choose to follow guidelines and take your core courses, such as English 101, College level Mathematics, Physical or Biological Science, Foreign Language, and another course, commonly referred to as a Free Elective, you don't have to take them at 8:00 in the morning anymore if you don't want to.

Yes, you can now begin your day at 12 in the afternoon should you so choose. Then you can pause for an extended lunch period at 1 p.m. and resume classes at 3, 4 and 5. You don't even have to go to class every day. You can make your schedule for MWF (Monday, Wednesday, Friday) or TTH (Tuesday, Thursday). Hell you can even miss classes without a forged note or come late without having to stop at the office for a tardy slip, and you won't even get detention. Hooray for you! And a hearty congratulations on your new found freedom!

But, with freedom comes a lot of responsibility- a level of responsibility many of you may need a little help navigating your way through. Yes, you are free, but now you are responsible for making "need based" versus "want based" decisions. This transition is essential to your successful transition from a child to an adult, and a better indicator of how successful you will be at adulthood than your 18th or even your 21st birthday.

Shifting from want to need based decision making independently is an integral part of maturing that many fail to master. You may ask, what is the difference between the two types of decisions? I'll tell you. Need based decisions are often the ones that are least favored. They are the types of decisions that your parents, as responsible adults, must make every day-the ones that they have consistently bestowed upon you, until now. You are the product of a culmination of "need based" decisions and sacrifices that your parents made for you. Yet, they are the ones that you probably do not yet understand.

You are free! So, No! You may not *want* to go to class every day. And no one will be there to make you. And frankly many-not all or even most-but many of us (Professors) don't or won't care whether you come to class or not. But know that whether we confront you or not-**we will** remember.

We will not call your parents, nor will your parents receive an automated message from the University informing them that you were absent or late. Even if they call and ask, we are not allowed to provide them any information about your academic progress without a signed consent form- (FERPA) from, guess who- you. Yes, "you," must give us permission, in writing, to speak to your parents about your progress in school.

So, you may initially be led to believe that you don't need to go to class every day. That is until you find that you are ill prepared for a test, you missed turning in an assignment that your professor <u>will not</u> accept late, or you get your midterm, or worse, your final grade and were not given consideration in the extra point that you needed to pass the course (no matter how good the excuse, how big the tears, how loud the voice, how good the apple). So, in order to reduce this pessimistic possibility, you *need* to go to class-everyday-even if and when you don't <u>want</u> to.

Hold on! Now, don't close the book yet. I'm not taking away from your strength and your maturity, nor am I attempting to lecture you. I'm just letting you know how it really is. How do I know?

I know because I am your Professor and I've seen some of the papers that you could likely write should you not read the rest of this book. I remember not remembering faces to names in my grade book when I am sitting in my bed averaging grades and trying to justify giving an extra point for a C or just giving the D. Or worse, I do remember the faces and the names of those who only come to class sporadically, and then come in late, loud and unprepared when they do, sit in the back of the classroom, and fiddle with their cell phones- text messaging when they should be paying attention like they are "getting over" on me-when I'm now laughing as I exercise my right place the big fat red F that the student has earned on the front page of the exam that is worth 30 percent of their grade or in the final grade column of my grade book.

But more importantly, I know because I have been a college student for a very long time. Like you, I made my way through high school with great grades when I put my mind to it and mediocre grades when I goofed off. And trust me, no matter what your peers may say, mediocre is not good. But, I didn't get my first F until, guess when? My first semester freshman year! My grades were a B, a C, a D and an F, and that averaged out to a whopping 1.5 g.p.a (grade point average).

Yes, Dr. Zoe Spencer was on academic probation her first semester in college. Why, because I was simply not prepared for the transition. What I found was that no matter how many college prep courses or advanced placement courses I took in high school, the academic process was not the same in college. And in spite of how mature and ready I thought I was, I wasn't. And I was still living at home with my Mama.

I found that there were fundamental things that I was just not prepared for and they impacted me academically and emotionally. I must have cried for weeks looking at those grades and that academic warning, because it wasn't like I had goofed off-okay well maybe some when I didn't show up for my 8 o'clock Psychology course (the D). I worked hard. Okay, well maybe not as hard as I could have. I studied hard. Well, at least when it was convenient and didn't pose a challenge to the other things I had going on in my life. I wrote what I thought were good papers, papers that I know Ms. Donnelly (my AP English teacher) would have given me A's on. But I still ended my first semester with a 1.5.

So, I am writing this book, not to berate you, but to prepare you, to give you the tools that you need to ensure that you don't end up with a 1.5 in your first semester

like I did. So read it carefully, take notes even, refer to
it when you need to, and share it with your friends if they
don't have one. And in the end, if you still have
questions email Dr. Z (zspencer@vsu.edu).

CHAPTER I

YOUR FIRST WEEK OF CLASS

Your first day of each class is extremely important. Although you may not be given much work, this is not a free day. So do not let any misled and/or misguided upper classmen convince you that it is, and do not miss it. It is essential for- and to you.

You see, on the first day, each of your professors will hand you a syllabus, pronounced (sil a bus). It should be a requirement-and is a very important and fundamental aspect of the course. Do not lose, destroy, ignore, or throw this away. It is your course guide-a course contract between you and your professor that delineates the objectives, requirements, dates, and expectations of the professor and the course. It binds both the student and the Professor-and will be essential if you ever have to challenge a grade.

Unlike high school, where your teacher gives you assignments daily, in college we (Professors) are responsible for letting you know what you will be required to do in advance. So, this syllabus is an outline of what you will have to do for the entire semester. It is a calendar that should give you the objectives of the class, the expectations of the professor, what you should have learned when you complete the course (learning outcomes), the readings, the assignments, their due dates and their worth, and the important dates and policies of your respective department, school, and the University, including the last day to withdraw from a class without a grade penalty.

Do you see why it is important? From this document you will be able to gauge how much work you will have to do for this class, and the next one, and the next one, and the next one. Now, it is not that I am trying to promote laziness. But, understanding how much work you will have to do, i.e. how many assignments are due and how they are spread out over the semester for each course, as well as the nature and extent of the assignments-whether they are subjective or objective, term papers or research papers, 3-5 pagers or 10-12 pagers, is very important in the grand scheme of balancing your course-load, especially in the freshman year.

Quite frankly, as a professor and a parent, I do not advocate-and am vehemently opposed to freshman overload. I believe that is unnecessary and counterproductive to the transition process and the goal of retaining students. And while there are some very bright and prepared students that

11

can handle overload, it is oftentimes handled with great stress and sacrifice-unnecessary stress and sacrifice. I argue that it is enough for freshmen to *have* to take required core courses that can be very challenging in the first year. So, to overload those core courses with either advanced core courses, or electives that are more rigorous than the core courses can be counterproductive to the adjustment and transition processes that all freshmen go through.

Freshman retention rates across the nation support the statement that freshman year can "make you or break you." So in aiming for the "making," it is important to review and evaluate each course syllabus so that at the most you will be able to effectively prepare and, if need be, make modifications to your schedule if necessary. I will pull all of this together in a minute.

Your professor will usually take the first day to go over this syllabus with you. Now, I know that y'all can read, otherwise you probably wouldn't be in college. But, don't take what seems to be an elementary formality lightly. Know that you can and will learn a lot about your professor and the course ahead by just listening, observing, and evaluating his/her presentation.

As your professor is reviewing the syllabus, he/she will most likely be expressing a part of their teaching personality by letting you know what is important to them, what they expect, what their peeves are, how lenient or rigid they may be etc. etc. But, they will also be revealing personality by letting you know what type of demeanor they have. From that you will be able to make a quick judgement on how well you feel you may fare with this professor and this course. This is your time and opportunity to positively use the "new found" control of your life and space to evaluate your professor and take charge of your academic experience.

This is a part of your new-found freedom. Unlike high school where your schedule is handed to you with no room for change because one teacher teaches one subject for all students, college is different. Because of the high volume of new freshmen who must all take the same required/core general education courses, you will have the "professor/course/time option." That means that there will be multiple sections of the same course that are being taught by different professors. Evaluate and make a decision. But, once you make a decision you must follow through diligently. This is what I mean.

First, you should always ask questions. Most colleges have a freshman orientation of some sort. They also have a group of peers that are responsible for mentoring incoming freshman. If there is an orientation, go! When you go, ask questions. If there is a mentoring group or association, find them, and when you do, ask questions. All freshmen, no matter what major they choose, must go through the same core courses- which means that they may have taken courses from the same professors that you will soon meet. So, you have the opportunity to seek the guidance and expertise of those who came before you. Don't be shy, ask questions.

Now some of my colleagues may get mad at what I am about to say, but I have to say it because this book is for you. Listen carefully. Students! Understand that professors are human too, and **we** come with our own sets of issues-good and bad, valid and invalid. Truth be told, some of us are more adjusted than others. And there are some of us, who are just plain off. But tenure and unions protect us and make it difficult for us to be held accountable for our failures and be moved so that energetic, passionate, and committed professors can take our place when we settle in too deeply. So remember this and do not relinquish your control by failing to ask questions and taking the student evaluations that you will receive lightly.

Anyway, back to the point, I argue that most of us truly want you to learn. Most of us have the greatest intentions. But how we go about teaching you can and will vary, drastically. Some of us will understand and be empathetic to the fact that you all are going through a major life transition, and that our courses are just one component of your entire academic experience and a smaller component of your entire lives. So while we need you to grasp the understanding that is necessary to successfully complete our courses, we don't need you to develop an ulcer as a criteria for getting a C. Sadly, though, some of us are not so understanding. In defense of my profession though, this is not to say that the Professor who gives you an A for mediocrity is a great professor, or one who requires you to achieve excellence in order to receive an excellent grade is a jerk.

However, I must admit, in fairness to you, that there are always a few of us who make it our mission to create the ultimate masochistic course in order to satisfy some internal or personal deficiency that we have not yet addressed or to make our classes a hazing process that makes us feel better about the hazing that we received in our Ph.D. program or dissertation defense.

Now I am not talking about those of us who will force you to reach your highest potential and will not let you be lazy or mediocre in our courses. Nor am I talking about those of us who, out of concern for the academic and intellectual development of our students, structure our courses in a manner that will prepare you all for advanced level courses and/or even graduate school. I am talking about "the masochists."

Let me give you some warning signs. If no one is signed up for a particular course, think twice. There is usually a column, if online, that informs students of the total capacity, how many people are enrolled, and how many slots are left. If it looks like this- 30 2 28. Warning! Achtung! Cuidado! It's like going to a barbershop or beauty salon and there is one barber/beautician who doesn't have any clients in the chair or waiting. Unless they are eating lunch, you can assume that they can't cut or style. Don't sit in the chair-even if you are in a rush- or you may not want to leave the shop when he/she is done.

This same principle can be applied to the course. If there are only two masochists who appreciate the masochistic experience- that means that most students do not like the experience, have been told about the experience, and/or would rather wait to get another professor/course than to attend that one. Unless you too are a masochist, do...NOT...sit...in...the...chair. Second, if the course syllabus looks **abnormally** rigorous, don't take the challenge if you don't have to. I'm not saying not to challenge yourself, or implying that you should always or only "take the easy way out," but the first semester is not the time to take unnecessary plunges/chances/risks if you don't have to. I did that in my political science course and that is where the F came from. There were 23 F's and 2 D's for that course, um...out of 27 students. Lastly, if during his/her presentation and introduction to the course, a professor lets you know up front that either he or she does not give A's or no one EVER gets an A in his/her class, don't call his/her bluff, you- will- not- win! I have had many debates with colleagues like this---and YOU- will-not!-WIN.

Know that for those types, a B will be reserved for the top 1st to 3rd percentile and above (those are the students that have done better than 99-97 percent of the class), the C's will be reserved for the above average students, the D's will be for the average students, and the instructor will feel very comfortable giving as many F's as he/she wants and students earn with no compassion with no argument. In college, getting a "grade change" is limited to extreme cases-and often requires the professor's consent. So ask, listen, and analyze. And if you see the warning signs-Do Not Enter.

After you have attended all of the courses, gotten a feel for each of your professors, and reviewed your course syllabi, you can sit down and ask yourself some very important questions. The main question is will you be able to reasonably, not easily, not even comfortably, but reasonably, be able to handle and succeed in each of your courses? If the answer is yes. Good and good luck! Be diligent, work hard, and proceed to the next chapter. If the answer is no. Don't panic, you have some options.

If you get the "nutty professor," you may want to consider selecting another course. If you have 3 MWF courses where you have hefty and objective assignments due each class, and 2 TTH courses where you have hefty assignments due each class, you may want to consider some revisions such as adding a less rigorous course (that I refer to as a "pad course"), dropping a course etc. Think critically, objectively, and responsibly and most importantly meet with your advisor to discuss your options.

WAIT! CAUTION! Before you commit to making changes you must know your add drop period. This is the only period where students are able to make changes, both additions and drops without any penalties, and it usually only lasts for the first week of classes. Knowing this is essential because in order to be considered full time, financial aid stipulations require that you maintain at least 12 credits to be considered full time. If you drop a course and fail to add another, you may risk falling below full time status and may suffer detrimental consequences with financial aid, scholarships, stipends etc. So be sure to discuss ANY changes with your academic advisor and ensure that you are within this period before you make any changes.

Please note that while most colleges require you to consult with your academic advisor before making any changes, many times students are inadvertently allowed to omit that process by being able to register for courses on line. I strongly advise all students to consult with their advisors to ensure that they do not make changes that could cause delays in graduation or adversely affect their academic progress/standing or hinder their financial aid. So know who your advisor is and make sure you make an appointment to discuss your schedule with him/her before making any decisions and before your senior year.

Further, understand that many courses have pre-requisites-which means that in order to take English 102, students must first complete English 101. Often times, sequence courses are not taught each semester. For example, English 101 may only be offered in the fall semester and English 102 in the spring. This means that if you do not take 101 in the fall, you will not be able to take 102 in the spring semester and will fall behind one year. So, before you do the finagling that I am about to suggest, please make sure you that you consult with your academic advisor and receive the appropriate guidance.

Disclaimer: (Dr.Z will not be responsible for any problems that may incur if this advice is not taken.)

Before you drop a class, you have to research what other courses are not only listed but "open." Just because a course is listed in the catalog does not mean that it will be open when you choose it. If you look online and it says 30 30 0, that means that there are no open slots. Do not drop your course for this one. What usually happens is that the word spreads about the "good courses" and "the good professors," so their courses fill up quickly and may be closed when you are trying to make changes to your schedule.

Before you drop a course, you must make sure that an alternative is open because should you drop a course and find that the other is closed, you could risk losing your original course spot and having to go through some heavy formalities to get into a course that may be worse than the original, or not being able take the course at all. So, before you touch your schedule, do what? Consult with your advisor and research first. Unless a course has received good ratings, you may want to research that course, maybe even attend that course if it is feasible to make sure that you will not be jumping from the pan into the fire. Once the add drop period is over, you will be stuck with what you have. So take this time period seriously and choose wisely.

If you find that you have an overload schedule, you may want to consider having what I term a "pad course." What I'm saying is that you should have one course that presents minimal stress. So, if you have chosen an Art Appreciation course that the professor in his/her own complex, is determined to "legitimize" by making you do more work than Analytic Writing 500 and Pre-calculus, maybe you should consider dropping that course and taking

Beginners Yoga. Take a course that will allow you to breathe and give you a respite from the rigor. Just because the course says Art, Music, P.E. does not mean it is a "pad course."

This is the importance of your first week in school.

I have illustrated some very important survival tips. (1) Research courses and professors before registering. (2) Make sure you set a good course schedule. (3) Don't abuse your ability to come to class late or miss classes without parental intervention. (4) Make sure you attend class on the first day. (5) Thoroughly review your syllabi. (6) Do a pre evaluation of your professors. (7) Once you have gotten all of your course syllabi sit down and evaluate whether you will be able to balance your courses and be successful in your first semester. (8) If you find that you have chosen a course or courses that may be overwhelming, consider changing your schedule. (9) Should you decide to change your schedule, consult with your academic advisor, research alternatives, make sure alternatives are available, 10)be sure to complete change during add drop period, and 11) make sure to make changes according to rules and keep copies of all documentation. Oh did I mention, consult with your Academic Advisor.

CHAPTER II

SUCKING UP

If anyone ever told you that sucking up wasn't cool, I'm here to tell you it is. Now I'm not saying that you have to bring your professor an apple every day and answer every question, because that can get annoying. But there is a level of, let's call it, "class participation," that is very beneficial. Why? Because the more you participate and engage in the material and discussion, the more noticeable you will become to your professor. And that's a good thing. At least for most of us it is.

Now before I begin, let me, at least forewarn you. There are a few of us, a very few, that don't want you to say a word or ask any questions in class. Now my colleagues may get mad at me again, but you know what I say. I have to tell it like it is.

There are a few of us who, in our own insecurity or attempt to maintain a concrete dominance, control, and authority over the classroom, rebuke any form of participation or questions during lectures. In this case, you have to be careful because these types may take your participation as an attempt to challenge and/or disrespect them and their process. You will be able to figure these types out by their responses to questions and inquiries.

Should you get this type, know that the classroom is your forum and the learning is your process. So, ask questions when you have questions, just make sure you try to ask them a little humbly. Not that you should have to, but sucking up, especially in your first year, while you are trying to negotiate the system, can be beneficial. And although I am one who usually encourages challenge to authority, this isn't the time. When you are stuck in a course, the last thing you want to do is offend the classroom dictator with your insolence.

But for the most part, in my experience, I can say with certainty that most of us will appreciate questions and discussion, as long as they are relevant to the topic and subject. And I can personally say that I tend to fall in love with the student(s) who break the ice and stimulates classroom discussion. It makes it fun and more engaging for me.

Anyway, this is the "suck up" process.

(1) Where you sit is important. I know that it is tempting to come in to the classroom and sit behind everyone else. I know. I used to do it. But, I'm here to tell you that I keep fresh

deodorant in my desk and frequent nice body splashes and perfumes. I also keep a tooth brush and toothpaste in my desk and tend to drink water when I have long classes. So, I don't stink. Nor do I bite. Although when I get excited I tend to spit sometimes. Sitting in the front or near the front makes a statement. That is, "I am not afraid of my professor because I am going to come to class prepared." So, I am always amazed and impressed by the person who sits in the first, second, or third row. That is why the suck ups get there early to get a front row seat. They know this. So, while the cool kids think they are the smart ones, they are not. And, I find that just like the statement, the students who sit in the front are, in fact, most often the most prepared and interactive. I guess if you sit in front you have to be. I remember their names and often look forward to seeing them. And when they are absent, I am often more concerned than anything else.

(2) Come to class prepared. There are most often readings that go along with class lectures. Although you should read the entire text, even if

you don't, you should do a thorough "skim it"
(generally of the highlighted terms etc.) or read
the main parts thoroughly and have at least two
questions prepared. This works in every class.
It shows the instructor that you have read, we
may not know how much, but knowing that you
cracked the book is oftentimes good enough for
us. Then, once you ask your prepared questions,
the professor will be less likely to call on you
arbitrarily. Control your space, don't get
caught in an embarrassing situation where you are
asked a question that you should know but weren't
prepared for. Now if you read thoroughly, like
you are supposed to, then you won't have to worry
about it, because either you will know the
answer, or be able to confidently say, "Yeah, I
was reading about that, but that was one of the
things in the text that I didn't understand."
But, not only that, make points and connections
in class and ask other impromptu questions in
class to show that you are connecting to the
material. This is always good.

(3) Don't view your professor as a leper. Don't be
afraid to approach your professor after class to

ask questions, explain situations etc. Let them
know what's going on in your space. Now I'm not
saying that you should view them as a confidante.
But, if you have some weaknesses in certain
academic areas, let them know up front and ask
for their guidance. If you are going to be
absent or late and you know in advance, let your
professors know this. If you are going through
some stress that may affect, or be affecting your
work, let your professors know this. There are
several reasons why. First, if a professor knows
that you have an academic limitation, for example
English as a Second Language… we may be more apt
to give consideration in grading your work. And
if not, we may give a more in depth critique to
help you to improve, or even volunteer to work
with you. If we know that you are going to be
absent or late up front, we will be less likely
to assume that you are simply being
irresponsible. And if you are going through
something, we will be able to guide you, perhaps
support you, and will, again, be more apt to give
you grading consideration. For example, if
Michelle has missed a day of class and she comes

to me and tells me that she is having severe family problems, and then she fails to come to class for the next couple of days, I would be concerned. I would, personally, try to reach her so that I could try to help her to, at the least, make the academic decisions necessary to help her to avoid major consequences. And if she asked for an Incomplete as opposed to the F, because we have discussed the issue and I knew, I would be more likely than not to give her that consideration. Most of us are human and understand that things happen and that your life is not just about academics. But don't take that for granted because we are also part time lie detectors too.

This is how you suck up. Why should you suck up? Well, if you are completely on point and you are getting all A's on your exams, assignments, and papers, you don't need to "suck up." Your work will speak for you. There will be no question. But understand, that as objective as grading is supposed to be, there is always room for the subjectivity that may make the difference between an 89 B+ and a 90 A- on a paper. And there's not much that you can challenge when that happens. Then there is always the class participation portion of the grade, that as a social science professor, I place great emphasis on. (This may differ for the hard sciences.) And that class participation (sucking up) percentage of your total grade is the justification that we give ourselves when averaging your final grade. It is the completely subjective portion of our scale. So, when you have an 87 average with exams, assignments and papers, and you have been key in the classroom, you get the A. When you've been sitting quietly in the back of the classroom, and your professor doesn't even know your name, you get the B. Do you feel me? So, go for the A.

CHAPTER III

CLASSROOM SKILLZ (SKILLS)

The academic transition from high school teaching and learning to college teaching and learning will require you to make some major adjustments. Unlike high school where you are given classroom assignments, you will find that the college classroom is a "lecture based" experience. Lecture, is where the professor stands in front of the classroom for most of the time and explains the material using visual aids such as the chalk board, power point, overheads etc. to facilitate the explanation. In most cases, there will be few classroom assignments. Some classes, especially the physical sciences, are even divided into lecture LEC and laboratory LAB. Where lecture is reserved for lecture, and lab provides the opportunity for hands on/practical assignments.

Many students are fooled into thinking that this is a boring process and sit doodling or drifting off to sleep or into countless daydreams never thinking that there is a reason and a process that they must adjust to quickly if they are to stay afloat. This includes active listening, integrating readings with lectures, and taking good notes.

Understand that your professor has prepared each and every lecture. He/She is not only drawing from his/her knowledge, but he/she has also taken the important points from the readings and other materials and incorporated them in his/her lecture. What your professor presents during lectures is the material that he/she wants you to know. So, if the teacher prepares the lectures, which reflects points that he/she deems important, than you can bet your meal plan that those are the same points that your exams will be based upon. Now do you see the importance and relevance of this babbling?

Reading your book will not be enough for you to get a good grade on an exam. You must integrate the lectures into your process. You do this by active listening and taking good lecture notes. How do you do this? Let me tell you.

Active listening is a psychotherapeutic term that is used to describe a process where the listener is actually participating in and acknowledging participation in the listening process. Understand that listening is a process. So for the purpose of this book, we are going to use the term active listening to reflect listening as an entire sensory process. Seem difficult? It's not that hard.

Hearing, seeing, and feeling will be the three senses that you will utilize in this active listening process. To put it simply, you will hear what the professor is saying and the emphasis that he/she is placing on certain things. When does the professor's voice rise? When do they pause and look at the students to see who is writing it down? When do they say point blank, "you will need to know this?" During this process, you will see what they present and how they are presenting it. For example, what are they presenting on power point, or on the overhead, or what terms are they writing on the chalkboard? If they took the time to write it down, chances are- you should too.

Finally, through taking an active role in getting to know your professor and the aspects of the material that he/she finds valuable, you will soon be able to feel what is important.

So, that makes the taking notes section small. Of course you will not be able to write down, verbatim, each and every thing that your professor says, but through cultivating your active listening process you will know what is important. And if you find following the lectures in class difficult bring a recorder to class so that you can record and take notes from the recording where you can control the pace.

The rules are simple though (1) If your professor verbally emphasizes it, so should you. Write it down. (2)

If your professor has put it in writing in any form, so should you. Write it down. (3) If it relates or reinforces something that you have read in the text, write it down. And (5) if your professor tells you that it is important or tells you to write it down, write it down. The message is simple. Write stuff down.

So, I guess you know what that means right? So that we are clear, it means that you will have to come to each class prepared to be alert and engaged in the lecture process. This means that you will need to adhere to good sleeping, eating, and social habits and patterns. It also means that you will need to come to class everyday. And should you miss a class, you will need to have a buddy that has good classroom skillS that you will be able to get the notes you missed from. This will be vital to your success in the course.

READING SKILLZ (SKILLS)

When I was a graduate assistant, I remember sitting in one of the professors' classrooms. I sat beside this undergraduate student who complained to me about the outlines that the students were required to do, and how she had not done well on her exams. So, I asked to see her notebook. Her notebook was thick and it appeared that she was rewriting her textbook- word for word- as opposed to reading her text and then outlining or taking notes. Now, although I bashed the standardized test in the beginning, I will now hypocritically refer to it.

Most standard tests have a reading for comprehension section. Reading for comprehension is essential. It is essential that students be able to read and understand the premise of the readings, not just recite the words. When you recite the words without understanding the meaning, you are not truly reading. Reading is a form of communication that is designed to deliver information through written text. Therefore, if the reader does not gather the information, reading becomes useless. Thus, it is essential that the reader (you) be able to pick out and understand the important points.

Fortunately for students, most Introductory text books will bold or emphasize the important points in some manner. There is also usually a summary and discussion section at the end of each chapter-complete with the key terms found in the text, so that should make it easier. So, do not make the mistake that the student made. Read as thoroughly as possible and as you go through take notes of the important points-mentally and physically. Understand the topic of the chapter. What is the premise? (That means what is the point/information that the chapter is making.) What are the relevant theories and concepts? How do you define or explain those theories and concepts? And how do those concepts tie in to form the topic? Difficult? No.

Just as you are able to articulate and summarize what a movie was about after you've seen it, you should be able to do the same after reading the book. Just as you are able to pick out the highlights, the major points, the symbolisms, the tension, and the message in a movie-or perhaps even a 'good' book, you must read your academic books in the same manner.

Let's take an example. Say the topic is 'senses'- which could be a psychological, biological, or physiological topic. What are the senses? Taste, Touch, Smell, Sight, Sound. I will use *Psychology* 3rd *Edition* by

Hockenberry and Hockenberry as an example. So you would

read the 5 paragraphs on Taste. There is one bold word,

'taste buds.' If it is bolded than it is a point of

interest. Therefore, you would take notes on taste buds.

Then there are 5 words in italics sweet, salty, sour,

bitter, and yummy. If it is italicized it is a point of

interest. So, you should take notes on it.

Now if you apply the questions above, just given the

information that I provided from Hockenberry and

Hockenberry, how should your notes look?

They should reflect Taste as a relevant part of the

Senses, taste buds as one of the primary components or

concepts of taste, explaining or defining what taste buds

are and how they work. Then you would explain sweet,

salty, sour, bitter, and yummy, which are the types of

taste buds that tie into taste. Very basic, but very

relevant.

Now if you take notes from your readings in this

manner, you end up with very brief, straight forward, well

organized, and easily reviewed information. You don't end

up with a hand written version of the text book.

Having 10 pages of neatly hand written notes for a 12

page chapter does not mean that you have taken effective

notes. What it means is that you are either not 'really'

reading, or are unable to decipher the relevant information and have chosen to repeat and rewrite as opposed to read for comprehension.

Cultivating your reading skills is just important as cultivating your classroom skills. These are the components that will facilitate your preparation and performance on exams, assignments, and papers. You don't want to rewrite the book and be bombarded with a whole host of irrelevant verbiage that you will have to go over again. The purpose of reading is to get the gist of the information, the main points, an overall understanding of the information and processes. Your notes are a summary of what you've read, something that should remind you of the important points of the chapter when you go back to them. That way when it is time to study for the exam, as will be discussed in the next chapter, you can review the summary instead of rereading and attempting to absorb entire chapters in the book *and* in your notes.

CHAPTER IV

PREPARING FOR EXAMS

Understand me when I tell you that cramming for an exam is **not** good! You will not win, ever! *Preparing* for an exam is. <u>Cramming</u> is when you take notes and never revisit them until that 24 or maybe even that 12 hour time frame before your exam. Then in that short time, you attempt to "cram," memorize, and retain all of the information that you learned during that period. <u>Preparing</u> for an exam is an ongoing process that goes along with your absorption and integration of the material.

In essence, you should be trying to gain a working knowledge of the information as an ongoing process. This doesn't mean that you should try to memorize each concept for each course, but it means that you should really try to understand the material, make it meaningful to you. If you are able to gain a working knowledge of the material, a general knowledge, an overall understanding, then preparing for the exam will be much easier. Why? Because you will have less to store, retain, and recall from your short term memory the night before and the day of the exam. Subsequently, you will reduce accelerated levels of stress, tension, and frustration while you are studying. More importantly, you will reduce the risk of STMO (that is short-term memory overload); thereby, reducing the likelihood of coming down with a bad case of CRS (that is: can't remember shit) on the day of your exam and getting a poor grade. Do you understand what I'm saying?

By following the advice provided in Chapter II and III, you should have very good notes and very well organized notebooks for each of your courses. Since I haven't told you this already, each of your courses should have separate notebooks and folders. Your notebook should be organized in accordance with readings and lectures and the folders should contain any relevant handouts. Your text, unless it is a borrowed book, should be highlighted so that you can easily and quickly refer to the important information that you should have taken notes on. But, if you have taken good notes, you shouldn't have to refer back to your book. Your notebook and the relevant handouts should be the only things that you have to review in preparation for an exam.

Earlier in this chapter I mentioned that cramming was not good. So, why do we do this? We know on the first day of class when we are going to have exams, so why wait? Why frustrate ourselves? I suggest that you begin studying for your exam at least a week in advance-that is in addition to your regular review, depending on the number of chapters and/or topics to be covered. You should allow at least a day or two for each chapter or topic. You should review and rewrite your notes for retention and then you should quiz yourself or have someone quiz you on the key concepts. You should be able to articulate the overall processes and theories and be able to define key concepts. You should also be able to place the names of relevant people.

I suggest studying by topic or chapter because many students create long lists of definitions and theories and people and attempt to memorize them out of context. It is my opinion that being able to organize notes by topic and containing the concepts, theories, and people by topic will narrow the extent of the memorization that must occur. Here is an example.

I am a sociology professor so I will stick to what I know. There are three major paradigms in sociology Structural Functionalism, Symbolic Interaction, and Historical Materialism. There are names, concepts and theories that are associated with each of these three paradigms. You could do it like this.

Structural Functionalism

Historical Materialism

Symbolic Interaction

Karl Marx

Max Weber

Emile Durkheim

Latent function

Manifest function

Traditional vs. Rational man

Proletariate

Bourgeois

Conflict

In this case and out of context you are required to define and memorize each of these terms independently and without reference. However if you do it like this. Historical Materialism (also known as Conflict Theory in introductory texts):

Karl Marx

Conflict between working and ruling class

Proletariate-working class-those who sell labor power for wage.

Bourgeois-ruling class-those who own resources land, means of production control how profits are distributed.

Structural Functionalism:

Emile Durkheim

Society consists of structures that have certain
functions

    Latent function-indirect function

    Manifest function-direct function

Symbolic Interaction:

    Max Weber

        It is the process of human interaction that
promotes societal progress.

        Traditional man-concerned with status quo

        Rational man-concerned with creating more
efficient means of existence.

In this manner, you have placed the terms, concepts
and names under specific paradigms. So, if nothing else,
you will know that Weber will always be related to the
Symbolic Interaction paradigm. That Conflict Theory will
always be related to Marx, etc. This type of organization
will facilitate your preparation for exams, especially the
multiple choice, true false, and short answer exams that
you will usually have in your freshman year. So if you get
a question that looks like this.

Karl Marx developed the Structural Functionalist
paradigm. You won't have to recall who Marx is and what he
did, you will know that his placement is under the

Historical Materialist paradigm. So the answer is… False.
Do you see where I'm going here?

The way that you organize your notes is essential to
facilitating your preparation for exams. The more
organized your notes are, (and don't take my word, figure
out what is more easy for you), the easier your integration
and absorption of the material will be. The more you have
integrated and absorbed the material, the less you will
have to memorize. The less you have to memorize, unless
you are blessed with a photographic memory, the more likely
it will be that you do well on your exams.

In any event, knowing and understanding the material
as thoroughly as possible will be beneficial in any form.

CHAPTER V

TEST TAKING SKILLZ (SKILLS)

I can tell you how to prepare for an exam, but I do not have any real test taking skills to give. I still do poorly on any test, other than essays. But, there are plenty of books on test taking. If you have issues, I suggest you get a test taking book. I guess you can even refer back to those SAT prep courses or something. The way I figure, if you've done okay on the SAT, these college exams should be cakewalks, if-and only if- you are prepared. So, this is my advice.

(1) Prepare well. Doing so will reduce test taking anxiety.

(2) Know that you know what you know when you walk into the classroom.

(3) Do not attempt to cram in the moments before the exam. If you don't know it, you're not gonna learn it in the next few moments. Attempting to will probably increase the anxiety and may result in that overload that I was talking about.

(4) Take time to meditate and even pray before the exam. That's always worked for me.

(5)   When you get your exam take time to read over the entire exam before you begin. This will give you a feel for what the exam is all about, and you will be familiarized with common themes. Many times questions are repeated in different sections in different ways. Being aware of this will help. I'll explain in a moment.

(6)   Read the directions and the sentences thoroughly. Don't loose points because you failed to catch the curve balls that some of us throw at you. For example. Karl Marx did *not* develop Historical Materialism. When you read fast, you may fail to see the word not and mark the answer True which would be incorrect.

(7)   Do not copy off of your neighbor or talk during the exam.

(8)   Time yourself appropriately. Make sure you don't spend too much time on one question or one section. Make sure you give yourself time to finish.

(9)   If you get stuck on a question. Continue on. You may be likely to find the answer to that question or at least some critical clues in other sections.

(10) Don't be in such a hurry to finish. Finishing your exam first does not make you the smartest in the class. And even though your classmates may look at you with envy, you will probably not receive the highest grade. Take time to review your exam thoroughly. Look through your exam to ensure that you have answered every question.

(11) If you don't feel that you've done well, don't worry too much. It usually takes one exam for you to get used to the exams and the way your instructor grades. Once you get your exam back, if you haven't done well, you will have, and should take the opportunity to review with your professor and make the adjustments that you need to make to do better next time.

CHAPTER VI

WRITING A GOOD PAPER

This is perhaps the most important section of this book, writing a good paper. Why? Because writing a college level paper is completely different from writing a high school level paper. The techniques and formats are completely different. So, consequently, turning in a high school paper for a college course could be detrimental. It could lead to a poor grade or worse a formal case of plagiarism. And plagiarism is an extremely serious matter that could lead to failing a course, academic suspension, or even expulsion from the university. So, pay close attention here.

Like I've said throughout this book, you know exactly what you have to do and when it is due on the first day of class. Just as cramming is not good, neither is waiting until the last minute to do a paper, especially a term or research paper.

PROPER PLANNING

This is self explanatory. Preparing and planning for your paper is vital. The first task is to choose a topic. Your topic should be one that is both interesting to you and your professor and relevant to the course. Once you select a topic, you should discuss the topic with your professor so that he/she can give you appropriate feedback.

Your topic should be one that is broad enough to give you flexibility in how you want to approach the topic, but narrow enough that you can do a good paper in the required number of pages. For example, you don't want to choose Violence as a topic because it is too broad. However, doing a paper on Domestic Violence would be more appropriate. You see?

Either before or after you get your professors approval, you should do a literature search. The search will show you how much and what type of information is available on the subject. You want to make sure that you have sufficient material to support your paper.

Hold on a second, let me go back. Now I want you all to understand that there may be some subjective papers that you will have to write. Subjective papers are opinion papers or reaction papers. Most often, in these cases, you will have to read or review some material, be it an article, a book, a movie etc. You will then be required to write a paper in which you summarize what you read or saw and then you critique it. This does not mean that you say 101 Dalmations was about 101 dogs that got stolen. It was a good book or movie. I liked it. Your grade will be an F.

You have to give a thorough summary and then critique the content and the premise, and the way it was written or produced. Then you can state why you liked it, or not. Romeo and Juliet was a story about two families who allowed their familial conflicts to interfere with their ability to support and nurture love…In the end, they loose the children that they loved and were trying to protect… While this story was written in language that was not familiar and sometimes became a bit confusing. The premise and moral of the story was very relevant. The way the story was developed illustrated how parental dominance over their children can sometimes end in tragedy, dah dah dah dah dah. Get my drift?

Well, anyway, unfortunately for you, most of your papers will not be subjective papers. So, your professors will not be interested in your unsupported opinions or beliefs or personal experiences. The college experience is an objective and scientific experience. Please note: Until you receive your Ph.D. and begin to publish qualified and reviewed works, you know nothing! Do you hear me, nothing! You must ground your opinions in literature and facts. You must support your arguments with qualified literature. So, before you begin, you should ensure that there is enough qualified literature available to provide support for your work. If you find that there is not sufficient support, you very well may want to consider choosing another topic.

Once you are clear to proceed with your topic, you need to organize your research by first deciding how you are going to present it. If your topic is Domestic Violence, what approach to domestic violence are you going to take? Are you going to do a general overview, for example Domestic Violence in the United States? Are you going to narrow it down to The Impact of Domestic Violence on Young Children? Whatever the case, you need to know how you are going to approach your paper before you begin.

DEVELOPING A GOOD OUTLINE

Once you know where you are going with your topic, the next step is to develop a good outline. The outline is the skeleton, the foundation of your paper. A good outline will keep your writing organized and limit or guard against scattered and unorganized papers.

A general outline consists of an introduction, body-which can be divided into subsections, overall summary and conclusion. If you are doing a compare and contrast paper, the outline consists of an introduction, summary of first

component, summary of second component, the comparison (how
they are similar), the contrast (how they are different),
overall summary and conclusion. If you are doing a
reaction or critique the outline consists of an
introduction, summary of work to be critiqued, the critique
of work, reaction to work, and conclusion. From these basic
outlines, you can fill in the blanks.

So if you are doing a general paper on Domestic
Violence, your outline may look something like this if we
are keeping it simple.

I.   Introduction

II. Body
     A. Prevalence of Domestic Violence in America
     B. Who are the Victims
     C. Societal Response
         1.   Hospitals
         2.   Police
         3.   Court System
         4.   Support Networks for Women

III. Conclusion

SELECTING RELEVANT SOURCES

Once you have developed the outline you can begin what
will come to be called a literature review. A literature
review is a review of the sources that you have selected to
gather your information from. As you review the materials,
you should choose and either highlight or write down
relevant information such as statistics, data, quotations,

and other information that will support and strengthen your argument.

Remember, unlike High School papers, you will not and MUST NOT regurgitate or rewrite another source word for word. You will be developing your own argument or work and will be using the sources to *support* what you are saying.

So utilizing the outline above, if you are doing a paper on Domestic Violence, you should be gathering statistics and information on (1) the prevalence of domestic violence, (2) who the predominant victims are, (3) how police, hospitals, and the court systems respond to domestic violence, and (5) the support network that is available for the victims.

If you have gone through your sources and highlighted the information, once you start writing all you will need to do is integrate the information that you have selected as you go along. If you have written the information down, you should be sure to also include which book you got the information from and what page it was found on. This will help you later.

WRITING THE PAPER

Your introduction should consist of an opening statement, the reason why you have chosen your topic, the relevance of this topic to the subject or course that you are writing for, and an overview of what your paper will cover/discuss. The body of your paper is your argument and/or the facts and relevant information that you have researched about your subject.

If you are presenting several themes or subtopics in the body of your paper, I suggest giving each it's own subtitle and section to allow for a clear delineation of each of the sub topics. The conclusion is a summary of everything that you have written and your final words. So using the information above your paper may look like this.

Introduction

Paragraphs

Prevalence of Domestic Violence in America

Paragraphs

Who are the Victims

Paragraphs

Societal Response

Hospitals

Paragraphs

Police

Paragraphs

Courts

Paragraphs

Support

Paragraphs

<u>Conclusion</u>

Paragraph

This style reduces the need for having to develop smooth and clear transitions from paragraphs that cover one subtopic to another. When you have subsections however, it becomes even more important that your summary tie all of the pieces together, summarizing how each relates to the overall topic. So the first few sentences of your summary may look like this.

"Domestic violence is an issue that deserves continued attention, as it continues to plague society and its members socially, politically, and economically. Over recent decades social systems have developed more formal responses to the prevalence of domestic violence by creating internal protocols and policies that are more victim friendly. Hospitals, police departments, court systems, and domestic violence shelters continue to build stronger relationships in order to maintain a strong continuity in the response to domestic violence…"

Do you see how that one paragraph tied in all of the components of the body? How it summarizes how all of the components are related to the overall statement?

If you cannot tie the subsections in neatly, you may want to reconsider if the subsection that doesn't seem to match, is truly relevant to the overall topic, or whether you have inadvertently introduced a new topic. If you have introduced a new topic, delete it, as it will ruin the continuity of your paper.

The conclusion is just a series of statements that reinforce the relevance of your topic and shows and/or reiterates how what you have presented has done what you promised in your introduction. But remember, it is the last thing that your professor will read. So make it strong.

The last thing, the last paragraph or sentence, that your professor reads will be the last thing that is on his/her mind before she places a grade on your paper. So it needs to have an impact. Don't rewrite your paper in the summary/conclusion, but try to insert either a "heavy hitting" concluding paragraph or at the least a powerful last statement.

View your conclusion like an attorney's closing argument. A closing argument is designed to remind the jury of what they just heard from the attorney. It gives an overall summary of the facts in the case. But more importantly, the closing argument is designed to sway the jury, to leave that last and lasting impression. "If it doesn't fit, you must acquit." I don't have to ask if you remember that statement. *That* is an impact statement that will live in infamy whether you thought O.J was guilty or not. So make your summary impactful.

WHAT IS PLAGIARISM?

Warning! Read this very carefully because plagiarism is a very serious academic offense that can easily be avoided with proper guidance. Here is that guidance. Under copyright and property right laws, when an individual creates something, it is considered their "intellectual property." They own it because they created it. It belongs to them. Consequently, reproducing or using their property <u>in any form</u> requires their permission. Referring to their property in text-that is in your paper, requires giving them the credit and making reference to their work in the text. Otherwise, people will assume that it is your own creation-*you* made it up in your own mind. So simply, if you did not make it up in your own mind, you **MUST**, unequivocally, tell your Professors where you got the information and who you got it from. Just like in the street, citing is like a game of "he say, she say." We get it right in the street when we tell Linda that Malia said xyz. Why do we tell Linda that Malia said it? Simply, because "we" didn't. We gave credit to Malia as the source of our information. We may be telling it, but we got it from somebody else. Get it? Good. Give that same credit to the source of your information in your papers. If you do not, you have plagiarized.

Plagiarism is using someone else's material in your work without properly citing the work. Anything, and I do mean anything that you take verbatim or closely paraphrase from a source other than your own thought process or your own experimental research must be cited. Citing means that you either paraphrase or place what was taken in quotation marks and give the name of the author, the publication year and the page number. This includes facts and statistics taken from other studies, statements, theories etc. etc. If you got it from another source, cite it, simply. Tell the reader who said it. By doing so you will avoid the possibility of being charged with plagiarism and either receiving an F on the paper, receiving an F in the course, or facing academic expulsion. Please know that plagiarism is a VERY SERIOUS offense.

There are different types of citations. APA, the American Psychological Association, is perhaps the most common type. You can go online and find the different types of citations. But here is an example. "You will place a direct quote in quotation marks" (last name of author, year of publication). If you paraphrase what you have read, you should still give credit to avoid any misunderstandings (Spencer 2005). Or if you state that 60 % of college freshman do not know how to adequately site, you must give credit (Census Bureau 2002). In some cases, and depending on the style you use, you may be required to use a comma and cite the page number (Spencer, 2005:50)

This information will let the reader, in this case your professor, know where you have gotten the information. How will they know? Your bibliography or works cited page will further inform them.

In your bibliography or works cited section you will list all of the sources that you referred to or cited. If you have cited a work in the body of your paper, you must include that work in your works cited page. If there are other works that you have referred to but not cited in the body, you will include those works in your bibliography.

Again there are different formats, and frankly, most of us (professors) don't even know the appropriate format verbatim and often mix formats, but generally speaking especially for a freshman, most of us will first be happy that you are citing and have a Bibliography page, and be happy to see this type of format.

Spencer, Z. (2005). <u>So Your Going Off To College: Don't Forget Your Survival Manual For First Year Freshman.</u> Zoes Press. New York, NY.

So when we see (Spencer, 2005), we know what book you took the information from.

Should you not do this, it is considered plagiarism. Even worse, should you find a paper on line and use it, that would be considered the worse type of plagiarism. Don't risk it, because we <u>will</u> find it. And should we find it, you will more than likely be done! Fini! Finito!

Plagiarism is the most serious academic offense and will result in harsh consequences that may affect your ability to continue your education and receive your degree. Many students are not familiar with plagiarism and have been used to using other peoples work without appropriately citing in high school without consequence. That is why making this transition is important and must be made immediately. For more reference information you can visit the American Psychological Association web site to get the appropriate citation guidelines. Familiarize yourself with it, practice it, and use it in your research and writing.

FORMAT

Formatting your paper is simple. Most professors will inform you of how they want their papers formatted in the syllabus. If it is not found in the course syllabus, make sure you ask.

Generally though, most professors will not accept handwritten papers. Your papers should be typed, double spaced, 12 points and Times New Roman with 1 inch borders all around. It should not be bolded or italicized or in any type greater than 12 points. Do not try to make your paper longer by using bold and 16 point or placing borders around it, or using 2 inch margins. We will see right through it. Your pages should be numbered and should come with a title page that has the title of your work, your name and student id number, date, professor, course and course number.

And people, make sure you use spell and grammar check. It only requires the simple double click of your mouse on tools and then spelling and grammar. And it only takes a few moments. Performing this task will reduce the points that you may loose for incorrect spelling and grammar. This is especially important for any work that you do for English 101. Man created computers that are capable of editing your work, use the tool.

You should also keep all of your papers saved on disk
or micro-chip or whatever new technology you are using just
in case your paper gets lost. I must admit that I've lost
a few.

BALANCING THE SOCIAL WITH THE ACADEMIC

I am not going to take this opportunity to lecture you about the things that I am sure all of your family, community, and church members have already lectured you about. Don't drink. Don't do drugs. Don't have sex. And be a respectable young man or young lady, blah, blah, blah blah.

Like I said in the beginning, this is your freedom. And you are going to do with it what you please. But, remember, you have the challenge of treating your new found freedom with a great sense of respect and responsibility. How you handle your freedom will speak volumes about your level of maturity. The more mature you are, the better you will be at balancing that freedom with responsibility. No, that's not reverse psychology. That is a fact.

Mature young people recognize tomorrows beyond today. In essence, they recognize preparing for the future is more important than the impulses of the moment that the importance of the need is greater than the want. And in realizing that and incorporating that philosophy into their daily lives and mind sets, they will be further equipped with the drive and diligence that is necessary to make sound decisions. And making sound decisions is a sign of maturity. Do you understand that level of reasoning?

College is a major transition. It is also the most significant bridge to your future. It is the bridge that you must travel in your transition from adolescence to adulthood, from dependence to independence. How you handle this experience will largely determine what your future will look like. Setting that bridge on fire would be completely counterproductive to your own process. So, you have to maintain control over your process at all time. And if you choose to deviate you have to make sure that the deviation from the academic is a controlled deviation.

Getting high, in any form, is an uncontrolled deviation, because you give the power and control of your life to your bartender, supplier and the drug or alcohol itself. You may think that you control that process, but truth of the matter is, well…you don't. Get drunk, have a car accident and kill someone or die, who controlled that after your initial poor decision, you or the alcohol? Get high, go to a party and end up getting date raped or date raping, who controlled that after your initial poor decision, you or the drug?

Having unprotected sex is an uncontrolled deviation. You may think you control that process but once you make that connection, well truth of the matter is you relinquish the control. Have sex, without protection, get pregnant, get someone pregnant, or end up with a bad case of gonorrhea or HIV, who controlled that after the initial poor decision, you? No. Get my drift?

I am not trying to be pessimistic but these are real life and all too frequent occurrences. You can take my word, do the research that will support my word, or play roulette with your life and future. Whatever the case, the bed you lay in is the one you must make, you know what I mean.

It may not seem like it but, unlike your parents perhaps, I don't support the notion that college is or should be a strictly academic process. I don't support the notion that in order to avoid the potential pitfalls, you should put blinders on and proceed straight ahead without looking around, or even deviating from the course. But, again, the deviation has to be one that you maintain maximum control over.

What I'm trying to say is that you control the initial decisions, when you make a poor decision, you relinquish your control to the substance, biology, the police officer, professor, etc. etc. etc. And you will be the one to suffer the consequences of the poor decisions you make. I DON'T WANT YOU TO EVER GIVE YOUR POWER AWAY BY CHOICE! Simply.

On the converse, and on a more optimistic note, if you are mature enough to balance the social with the academic, the outcome could be very beneficial.

College is perhaps one of the greatest social experiences that you will encounter, especially if you are away from home and live on campus. It is a time of intra reflection, self definition, personal, and social growth. It is a time where you will forge new friendships and alliances, learn great lessons, experience memorable experiences, really begin to figure out and develop who you really are, and prepare for life after college. And frankly, I don't think that you can do this with your head and heart firmly buried in the books. Actually, I believe that burying your head in the books has the potential of delaying your social growth and integration. It has the potential of blocking your ability to develop and cultivate the social and interactive skills that will be essential to your transition from college to the real world.

So, I advocate taking the time to experience the social aspects of campus and community life. Attend college functions, sporting events and even parties. Attend meetings and at least evaluate organizations that you may want to become involved in after your freshman year. Not that you should or have to be involved, but should you choose to, know that your organizational and community involvement will be noteworthy additions to your virgin resume when you graduate from college. Use your freshman year as a period of social exploration and research.

More importantly, don't forget or neglect the things that you enjoy. Don't give up hobbies, make time. Make time to go to the movies, talk to your old friends, bowl, read for pleasure, jog, knit, or just relax. Whatever you like, do it. Don't allow the work to overcome you.

Keeping in touch and balancing the social with the academic is essential to promoting more healthy adjustments and transitions. It reduces the anxiety and stress. It also reduces the risk of situational or clinical depression, adjustment disorders and other psycho social issues that could potentially accompany your transition.

But, if you find that you are feeling any of the symptoms, such as trouble concentrating, sleep disturbances, changes in appetite, feeling blue, crying spells, disassociation from things that you enjoy, or just being in a funk that you are having difficulty getting out of, share your feelings with someone you trust. Most colleges and universities have a counseling center staffed by qualified mental health professionals and anything that you share is confidential. Know that seeking help doesn't mean you're crazy, so don't let anyone or you, yourself, place a label or a stigma on the process that may affect your willingness to seek help. O.k?

SUPPORT NETWORK

Know that there is a support system for you should you have problems. Make sure that you grab your student handbook. If not, the information should also be contained in your college website. But, for the most part, these are the key places that you should know. First, generally student insurance is included in your student fees as a part of your matriculation fees. If you do not have private insurance, either individually or through your parent's plan, make sure that you familiarize yourself with the student health insurance plan and procedure.

-Student Health Center- for all physical health problems, services should be free and covered in matriculation fees.

-Counseling Services- for mental health support.

-Office of Student Affairs- for student related problems.

-Office of the Provost- for academic and financial issues.

-Chair of the Department or Dean of the Department-for issues with professors or grades etc.

And if all else fails, call your mama and/or daddy, they'll handle it.

Or just ask Dr. Z.

PARENTS CORNER: A PROFESSOR MOM'S PERSPECTIVE

Dear Parents:

First let me begin by stating that I wrote this manual
for my son and god daughter when they went of the college
in 2005. But, I wrote this section from my observations
and communication with many students (your sons and
daughters) over the years. So, it is just my advice from
the perspective of an Auntie Professor who now gets to
nourish your sons and daughters while they are here.

So first, let me shout my sincerest congratulations to
you all on a job well done, and best wishes on not only the
success of your child in this next phase of his/her life,
but to leniency on your mind, body and pocket. If no one
else has patted you on the back, I do so now. Getting your
children through adolescence safely and in tact is an
accomplishment.

Many people do not realize that getting through the
teenage years with a decent relationship is perhaps one of
the most difficult transitions for children and parents.
It is a period where children are experiencing a wide range
of physiological/hormonal ebbs and flows that they must
adjust to, a wide range of social issues and pressures that
they must negotiate, and the delicate search for the

establishment and balance of their own self identity. And often times, as a result of the many changes that they are going through and the parents' attempts to negotiate those changes, it often becomes a time of conflict, resistance, alienation and rebellion in varying degrees. So, the fact that your children have made it to college, no matter how "expected" it was, is something to be celebrated. So, once again congratulations! Good job!

Now begins a new phase, a new transition- that is the transition from adolescence to adulthood, from dependence to independence, which will directly affect you. Yes, you. As your son or daughter is growing into him/her self, you will also have to grow into your new parental role. You too must make a transition from mother hen and papa hawk to a more passive role. You must now move from micromanager to division manager. Consider it a promotion, a promotion for everyone. Your son or daughter must now take a more active and direct role in managing his/her life, and you must be more of an overseer of that process.

This is your opportunity to trust in the guidance that you have given and the values that you have instilled and watch your children soar, dive, soar, dive, until they soon fly away from the nest all together. To watch this process occur without having complete control can be very difficult

if you are not prepared. However, continuing to thwart the
inevitable process by attempting to assert the same level
of pre 18 control that you used to could be detrimental to
not only your son or daughters development and transition,
but to your relationship as well. So, this transition, for
all, is not one to be taken lightly.

Granted for some parents, this transition will be more
easy than others. But now is the time when you will be able
to gauge and understand how mutual the parent/child
dependency really is. It's a different kind of dependence,
but a dependence nonetheless. Now is the time when you
will have to realize that you are no longer in control of
your son or daughters life. And perhaps, now is the time
that you will have to begin to redefine your role as a
parent in order to better support and further prepare your
child for his/her new role as a responsible adult.

As I am assuming all adults are aware, being a
responsible adult requires that aspiring adults be given a
strong foundation and then be given room to experience
life, which includes making both progressions and
regressions, achieving and making mistakes.

Making mistakes is a fundamental part of progress.
However, the possibility of making mistakes is one that
most parents have been trying to avoid "for" their children

for all of their children's lives. And perhaps, at this point, for a son or daughter to make a mistake would be something that many parents may take personally, if they have not yet made the adjustments and transitions that they need to make. That is why making the transition alongside your child is imperative.

Sadly, yet realistically, some parents may find that they have a codependent style relationship with their children. And in such, may find it more difficult, to let go, because the "letting go" means that they may not have the buffer that they've had in their relationships with their children for so long. They become our lives. But, remember, at this point, it is about ensuring that the children continue to receive the best guidance and support as possible, so that they may excel in school with minimal stress and ultimately become the productive citizens that we have prepared them to be.

"Let them go." Calling every second of the day and micromanaging them at this point will make them resentful and in some cases downright angry. And if they are away, the resentment may lead them to "cut you off" all together. Remember they are not upstairs in their rooms anymore, so they now have control over when, where, and how often they speak to you, if at all and how they negotiate their

"responses" to their conflicts with you. Caller id and
ring tones are now standard on most phones. Don't make
them ignore you.

     If you have developed a good relationship with your
son/daughter, trust the foundation that you have
established. He/She will come to you when they need you.
They will communicate with you when they need you and they
will share with you and answer any relevant questions.
They are going through major transitions in their lives, so
they don't need the extra pressure of your insecurities.
Give them the flexibility that they need to make their own
decisions. Yet, keep "in touch" with them. Allow them to
make the mistakes that are necessary to their growth and
development, while monitoring those that may be
detrimental. And when they make mistakes, don't take it
personally, don't be too judgmental, and don't get angry-
these reactions will alienate them and make them less
likely to share with you in the future. Instead, use their
mistakes as an opportunity to make the connections, use
them to teach the life lessons that you've probably been
trying to instill in them all of their lives. Their
mistakes will be more profound if we take a connective and
analytic, rather than a punitive approach.

Now that I've told you to let go, I will also tell you to "hold on." Understand that "let go" does not mean be blind and/or neglectful. Our jobs as parents are never completely done. So, letting go, simply means giving them room to grow, not holding on so tight. You must, of course, continue to communicate and keep "in touch" with your children, just on a different level. The parent child bond is solid, so continue to use parental instinct throughout this process. Show them that they are trusted and make that trust a gift that they are responsible for taking care of. But, always be aware of any significant changes in your child's behavior, attitude, performance, or daily routine. Be aware and on top of any changes that may indicate a problem, such as severe stress/or anxiety, depression, psychological disorders, substance abuse, or suicidal ideation, because this is the time that these things may be more likely to manifest.

Before your son/daughter leaves for college, make sure that he/she is prepared with information about the detriments of alcohol and substance abuse, date rape, depression and anxiety before they leave home. Maybe give them some hard core and impactful reality checks before they leave. For example show them articles etc. of the incidence and problems associated with excessive alcohol use and substance abuse on college campuses, such as date rape, alcohol poisoning and overdose etc. and give them the tools needed to avoid these situations. Know that these are the major problems that are too common on most college campuses. So, do your best to ensure that they don't get involved in them. But, know that once the information is given, once the lessons are taught, there are limitations in the level of control and involvement that parents will have. We have to let go.

Now that I have told you to let go and then hold on, I will tell you how to "hold on" without appearing to be "holding on." First and most importantly, be familiar with all of the guidelines and important dates of your son/daughters College or University, they are still young and probably will not be as responsible and diligent with dates and deadlines as we need them to be to be prepared. Know add drop periods, financial aid deadlines, other financial/housing/contractual deadlines, midterm and final exam dates, mid term and final grade dates etc., so that you will have the information that you need to quietly keep track of your son/daughters progress, and be "supportive" and/or confrontational when you need to. Because at the end of the day, as parents, we are still responsible for our children's collegiate and academic progress.

If you know the dates, you can ask questions and be parental at the appropriate times. Know that once your child gets to college, by law, as a parent you WILL NOT have any access to anything that has to do with your son or daughter. You WILL NOT be able to talk to professors, or access any of your child's records. You will be completely dependent on them to tell you, tell you the truth, or sign the waiver that allows you to do the above mentioned. In essence, you will be completely at the mercy of your son or daughter to gain the information about their progress.

So, it is imperative that you maintain a good working relationship with them so that they will feel comfortable communicating honestly with you.

CONCLUSION

I have given you just a basic guide, full of some
survival tips that I believe will help to make your
transition and adjustment a little smoother. But, don't
stop with this pamphlet, get other books on writing,
citing, taking notes, time management, test taking etc. so
that you will be even more prepared.

Know that it may seem hard at first, but hang in
there. It gets easier as time goes on. Work hard,
maintain a balance, and do the best you can. You've gotten
this far. Congratulations! And good luck with the rest of
your journey. I LOOK FORWARD TO SEEING YOU (AND YOUR
PARENTS) WALK ACROSS THAT STAGE IN 4 YEARS! HEY! NO MORE
THAN 5!

With Love,

Dr. Z.

CPSIA information can be obtained
at www.ICGtesting.com
Printed in the USA
FSHW010904201220
77046FS